***The Balancing Act
of A Busy Mom***

The Balancing Act of A Busy Mom

Happiness is the Key to Balance & Productivity

Melissa Harris

No portion of this book may be reproduced in any form without written permission from the publisher or author, except as permitted by U.S. copyright law.

This publication is designed to provide accurate and authoritative information regarding the subject matter covered. It is understood that neither the author nor the publisher is engaged in rendering legal, medical, or other professional services. While the author and publisher have used their best efforts in preparing this book, they make no representations or warranties with respect to the accuracy or completeness of its contents and specifically disclaim any implied warranties of merchantability or fitness for a particular purpose. The advice and strategies contained herein may or may not be suitable for your situation. You should consult with a professional when appropriate.

The Balancing Act of A Busy Mom
First Edition. July 2023.
Copyright © 2023 Melissa Harris. All rights reserved.
Publisher Vue Claire LLC.
Hardcover ISBN 979-8-9896316-0-5

To my boys—
who made me a mom
and taught me how to have a life.

Contents

Forward i

Introduction 1

Chapter 1 Embracing Your Happy Place 5

Chapter 2 Self-Love is Not Self-ish 11

Chapter 3 Organizing Your Life 27

Chapter 4 Productivity Tips & Tricks 37

Chapter 5 The Benefits of Balance 53

Chapter 6 Conclusions and Insights 59

Chapter 7 Continue Your Progress 65

About The Author 71

About The Publisher 72

More Information 73

Forward

As a woman, a mother, a former spouse, a boss, a co-worker, a daughter, a sister, a friend, I want to tell you – I see you. I understand the struggles, the joys, the isolation, the rewards, the frustration, and the sacrifice that comes with being an individual trying to make it all happen for ourselves and for our families. Managing a household, tending to the needs of children, husband, and often extended family members, having some semblance of a social life, and pursuing a full-time job or career is a lot to juggle. Many days we manage it like a superwoman. Other days not so much… We run "90 to nothing", not making the progress we think we should, stressed out mentally, at our wits end, and fall into bed exhausted to start it all over again the next day. I get it; I have been there. We all go through hair-pulling moments and dark times in our lives. No one is immune. And thankfully they do not last forever. We can learn and grow from those times if we allow it. And we can become better and stronger and wiser.

My story begins with a promising marriage, a blossoming career, and two wonderful children. And it transitions through a divorce, financial turmoil, mental depression, and raising those two wonderful children on my own. It then transitions again into a stable, balanced, and productive life. Not by chance, by choice. The lessons learned during those life transitions were invaluable. I would not be the person I am today without those experiences. And it amazes me that I can say that now! If you would have asked me 10 years ago, I would have said something very different (probably interjecting a few curse words), nor would I have believed that a positive outcome could even be possible. But it's true. And it is. And I want to share those lessons with you.

Achieving that place of balance in our daily lives begins with finding the balance within. And it begins with becoming happy and thankful in each moment. Finding inner peace and true happiness is not random. It is not a gift bestowed on you because "you've paid your dues" or "you are good person". It grows within you from a place of deep understanding and a practice of self-love. It manifests from a pure desire and a belief that you are worthy and deserving of good things. Our life stories may be different, but we are sisters in what we have endured and what we face every day, and we can be partners in the success of our next chapters.

Introduction

"There is no greater good in all the world
than motherhood.
The influence of a mother in the lives of her children
is beyond calculation."
—James E. Faust

One of the most powerful and satisfying experiences that any woman will ever have is motherhood. As mothers, we nurture and shape the lives of our children and our families. Of course, fathers play a vital role in the family too, but mothers are the true CEOs! They set the tone of the family. Their emotions, attitudes, and expressions directly affect how the family feels, communicates, and connects.

Sometimes, the responsibilities of a full-time career and household obligations can overshadow the fulfilment and joy that a mother feels when raising children. She may feel

Introduction

overwhelmed, often tired, and running around all the time but not accomplishing much (and always with more to do). She may not have time for things she enjoys, her hobbies, and spending time with her husband. She may feel like she is sacrificing herself for everyone else and no one else is doing the same. She may feel mentally exhausted and even resentful, angry, or depressed at times. Does this sound like you? It may come as a surprise, but you do have a choice to take steps to balance those family and work demands or to continue to let these demands overwhelm and drain you. Millions of women have learned to successfully and happily mix a career and family day in and day out. And you can too.

The goal of this book is to share eye-opening and effective concepts, like self-love, meditation, intentional prioritization, and tips for personal productivity, that you can incorporate into your busy life to improve your family-career balance and create long-term happiness and fulfillment. In these pages, you will learn…

- that tapping your inner happiness is the first and most important step to finding life balance;

- the necessity of self-love, what it is, and how it can change your thoughts about yourself;

- practical ideas to improve organizational skills, which is a vital component to real productive outcomes;

- simple action items that enhance the completion of duties and tasks, without burn-out, and maximize productivity (and they are not what you think); and

- recommended resource links to continue your personal growth journey.

In these pages, you'll find intriguing concepts and useful ideas to challenge your thinking in your current circumstances. This is not a one-size-fits-all, snap your fingers, overnight success book. It doesn't happen that way. BUT you can begin seeing positive results quickly if you consistently apply the principles, even for just a couple weeks. This is a book of victory, to empower working mothers of all ages to seek happiness, create balance, and improve productivity.

Chapter 1 Embracing Your Happy Place

"Whatever lifts the corners of your mouth, trust that."
-- Rumi

Your happiness is a priority. Read that again...
YOUR HAPPINESS IS A PRIORITY!

Oftentimes, this idea is the hardest hurdle to overcome. We are so used to giving to and providing for others' needs that we put our own needs on the backburner. Until something happens that requires us to look at that backburner – a burn-out, an illness, an accident, a mental breakdown, or a realization that something deep within us is missing.

Everyone is deserving of happiness and so are you. You must choose to make your happiness real in your own life. You are the only one that can. Joy, thankfulness, contentedness is a choice. It flows from the inside out, not the outside in. It is cultivated within us; it cannot be handed to us by someone else. It is not someone else's responsibility to make us happy – it is our own.

What is true happiness anyway? It is personal. It can be described as a deep appreciation, peace, and contentment; and it can also be described as excitement, joy, and a zest for life. It *feels* different for every individual and can be triggered through many different thoughts and experiences.

Happiness is not just about taking action that makes you feel good in the moment, though that may be part of it. It is that fine inner balance and self-knowing that allows you to be your most fulfilled self through all life's experiences and in all life's roles. True happiness is not static but a continuous evolving state of the heart and mind. It is more than a once-in-a-lifetime or a once-in-a-while event. Thoughts and experiences that create positive feelings of pleasure and joy release endorphins in the brain, which are felt in the body, and which can perpetuate calmness, peace, and bliss. We can learn to sustain those feelings of happiness through our daily attitude and gratitude. It is a conscious choice we make every day.

What Exactly Is Happiness?

Definitions of happiness vary between psychologists, scientists, ministers, and motivational speakers, however certain descriptive words are common throughout them all:

- ❖ a state of well-being and contentment
- ❖ a pleasurable or satisfying experience
- ❖ characterized by or indicating pleasure, contentment, or joy

Consider these words:

Joy	Blessed
Pleased	Exhilaration
Glad	Contentedness
Cheerful	Satisfaction
Blissful	Peace

…just to name a few. Speak them out loud right now and reflect on the feelings that they conjure in your body and the pictures that they paint in your mind. Those words just feel *good*. And that is the basis of all happiness – feeling good.

Happiness may have different meanings to different people. And they are all right! Ultimately, living a life aligned with your values, finding joy in simple daily activities, and just feeling good are all keys to developing genuine lasting happiness. In our own special ways, each of us define our happiness. We are the only ones that can!

In our current society, true happiness seems elusive. The definition of success has changed and continues to. It is now associated almost exclusively with fame and wealth. To "fit in", demands and expectations of people have expanded to dangerous levels. New generational ideas are forming, cultural norms have morphed, technology has grown exponentially over the last 20 years, and the world has become smaller and bigger at the same time. The pressures to look perfect, act perfect, have the perfect career and the perfect family can be overwhelming. What we see versus what we believe and how we choose to live our lives must be revisited.

There has been a spotlight in recent years on the dramatic increase in physical and mental health issues. Social media influences and "trying to keep up with the Joneses" mentality has created a comparison culture. Extremist political and religious views across the world have divided people, even within families, into factions against each other. Finding balance and true happiness in this environment is different than it once was. It forces us to look within and define ourselves – not to someone else's "rules" but to our own.

Achieving your own personal bliss is about rethinking your reactions and behaviors and developing a more positive mindset, despite what may be going on around you. We hear a lot about the "abundance" mentality these days, but the teaching is far more than just about wealth and money. It is a deeper concept of the mind and heart that affects all aspects of our being. Abundant thinking (as opposed to scarcity thinking) involves embracing the idea of choosing positivity over negativity. Focusing on what is good, and not dwelling on what is not good, raises your energy frequency and draws beauty into every area of your life, starting with your inner being. There are many wonderful teachings and books about positive thinking and affirmations, the laws of frequency and attraction, and abundance, so we will not go into the depths of those concepts here. Know that there are resources out there to help you change your mindset and usher in more balance, peace, and joy into your human experience. Some of those resources are included in Chapter 7.

Genuinely positive people naturally develop habits and make conscious choices that help them lead happier lives at work and at home, even in the midst of stress and difficulties that we all face. It is indeed possible to live a life of genuine happiness, and you can too.

Chapter 2 Self-Love is Not Self-ish

Often we are reluctant to promote self-love
mostly because we confuse it with selfishness.
Since we are humans, we ought to have a
healthy love for ourselves;
it is from this fount that love flows out to others.
—Mason Olds

If true happiness develops from within, then where do you start if this feeling is not part of your daily experience? How do you become happy? You must have the willingness and the courage to look inside yourself and do the inner work to change your thoughts and attitudes. You must prioritize you. Sometimes you must put yourself first.

This premise often goes against the grain of our traditional thinking. We were raised to put others first. We were taught not to be selfish. Our examples growing up were those mothers, grandmothers, aunts, and friends that went above and beyond for their families and communities, sacrificing themselves for the wellbeing of others. And often they paid the price for it, whether it was noticed or not, in their physical, mental, or emotional health.

In earlier generations, women often suffered in silence because they (1) were expected to repress their emotions ("don't be so dramatic", "big girls don't cry"), (2) were told to make themselves small or unseen ("be still and quiet", "just do what you are told", "don't talk back to those in authority"), and (3) were not encouraged to follow their dreams ("you're not smart enough", "it's a cruel world out there", "just find a husband who will take care of you"). They could have been more, but yet they did not know how to become more. They abided by the rules of their generation and compromised themselves for the sake of others.

Not all women were raised this way or had these experiences, of course. And make no mistake, choosing to be a stay-at-home parent, and not working outside the home, is a valuable and worthwhile calling. However, there were many women that felt they could not break free of such a life that was imposed on them. And maybe there are still some that feel that way today.

The quote at the beginning of this chapter is profound and explains, in a nutshell, what self-love is and what it isn't. Self-love, in its purest form, is accepting your own worth and value; properly nurturing your own well-being and happiness.

Other spiritual sources support the idea of loving and taking care of yourself just as you love and take care of others:

"And you shall love the Lord your God with all your heart, with all your soul, with all your mind, and with all your strength.'
This is the first commandment.
And the second, like it, is this:
'<u>You shall love your neighbor as yourself</u>.'
There is no other commandment greater than these."
--Mark 12:30-31 NKJV [emphasis added]

Self-love is not arrogance, conceit, narcissism, vanity, pride, or elevating yourself above anyone else. It is acknowledging that YOU are just as important as other people. As your spouse. As your partner. As your children. As your boss. You deserve to take care of yourself, just as you take care of others. It is not about taking care of you as one and only; it is about taking care of you **also**. We must remember we cannot truly give what we do not have. If we are depleted - physically, emotionally, spiritually, or mentally - then we have nothing good to give anyone. We <u>can</u> share with others positive aspects that we have cultivated in ourselves. We, particularly as women, need to develop a more open mindset about how we see ourselves. Balance, fulfillment, and happiness are vital principles that we must embrace for ourselves, for the benefit of our families, our careers, and our communities. That is not selfishness; it is necessity.

What does it mean to love yourself? And how do you do it? First, consider how you show love to others. Most people subconsciously do for others as they would want others to do for them.

My mother loves to bake. One of her favorite baked items are cookies. She has probably made every type of cookie that has ever existed over the course of her lifetime (only a slight exaggeration!). She makes cookies and gives them away. To every family member in her vicinity. To the minister at church. To neighbors. To the mail carrier. To patients she visits in the hospital or nursing home. Everyone in the community at one time or another has enjoyed my mother's cookies. And, to this day, one of her most favorite gifts to <u>receive</u> is homemade baked goods! You would think she would be so sick of looking at cookies that she would prefer other types of gifts, but she doesn't. It just goes to show you that people give to others what they themselves would like to receive from others. I'm sure you can prove this statement true even in your own life.

How you treat others and how you give of your time, attention, kind words, and assistance is how you should treat yourself. If a friend came to you upset or grieving, you would not ignore them or say "Just get over it". You would lend a listening ear, a shoulder to cry on, and encouraging words. When we, ourselves, are feeling upset, grieved, or stressed, how many of us talk harshly to ourselves, or even ignore these feelings and needs and bury them? This is not healthy.

It does not take other people to lift us up or tear us down. Our own self-talk can either help us or hinder us. Self-talk is that internal mind voice, that chatter, the consistent ruminating in our own heads. And we talk to ourselves all the time, whether we realize it or not! The next time you find yourself thinking, analyzing, deliberating, replaying experiences over and over in your head, consciously recognize that you are doing it and *listen* to what you are saying to yourself. Is it positive or negative?

I have had a perfectionist personality most of my life. Which also means that I have been very hard on myself when I wasn't "perfect". Even as a child, I would strive for the best grades in school and would organize my room just so with everything in its place. As a young adult, my make-up and hair would have to be perfect every day. I expected to be top of my high school class upon graduation. If I didn't meet others' expectations, and my own, I would become upset and depressed. As I matured and became more self-aware, I began to realize some of the negative thoughts that I was telling myself. In times of embarrassment or when I made a mistake or didn't meet someone's expectations, I would have detrimental thoughts like "I am so stupid. Why did I do that? I'm a failure. I'm no good at this. I'm making a fool of myself. I can't do this. I just need to stop trying." Etc. Etc. Many of us say these types of things to ourselves without realizing how debilitating they are. Negative thoughts perpetuate anxiety, low self-esteem, and depression. When I recognized this, it was a lightbulb moment for me. I became more conscious of what I was saying to myself, particularly in times of stress, and I made an effort to stop speaking negative statements about myself. I replaced my self-talk with positive uplifting words. When I caught myself using the word stupid,

I would immediately say "No! I am smart and strong". I didn't necessarily believe those positive statements at the time I said them, but I stuck with it. Within a matter of weeks, those negative thoughts I once had were almost completely gone. My outlook changed, my self-esteem increased, and I started seeing myself as a worthwhile and valuable person. I wish I had had this epiphany earlier in my life. It would have saved me much grief. It was life-changing!

Consciously tuning in to your self-talk and making the choice to shift it can change your life too. Even if you don't feel like it is the truth yet, say the good things about yourself anyway. You may have to "fake it till you make it" for a while. You are re-programming your mind and it takes time to overcome those old, ingrained beliefs about yourself.

Your thoughts create your world. Make those thoughts positive and they will work for you, not against you. This is the first step in learning to value yourself, which is a key step to developing long-term inner happiness.

Self-love not only includes how you think and feel about yourself but also how you take care of yourself – mentally, physically, emotionally, spiritually. Self-care is an essential aspect of self-love.

Don't be so hard on yourself.

Everyone makes mistakes or not-so-great decisions sometimes. We are all human, and this life was meant to provide contrast and choices for us. A mistake is not always bad if you learn and grow from it. So, give yourself a break. Keep the long-term big picture in mind and don't overreact to the small stuff.

Treat yourself as you would treat others.

Remember, you are just as important as other people and deserve the same care and treatment that you give to others. Be conscious of your self-talk. If you wouldn't say it to someone else, don't speak it to yourself. Exercise compassion and patience with yourself every day.

Do at least one thing just for you each day.

Set aside time, even if it's just a few minutes, every day for yourself to do something that you enjoy. It can be something as simple as reading, taking a walk, soaking in the tub, or taking some quiet time to pray or meditate. If you love to knit, make time to knit. If listening to music lifts your spirits, then do it. If you have a favorite TV show, dedicate the time to sit and watch an episode. Allow yourself some me-time every day. It will not only reduce stress but will begin to establish balance in your life.

Develop yourself. Grow mentally, physically, and spiritually.

The best investment you could ever make is investing in yourself. If there is a skill that you would like to learn, online classes or books are available on virtually any subject. Having interests and hobbies, developing your gifts and talents, and creating life-long goals is important. Remember, your kids will grow up and leave the house one day. Plan for that.

Create A Desires List.

In 2020, I was inspired to join a Mindvalley online course that walked each participant through identifying our desires and goals in several life categories, such as health, career, family, love relationship, finances, etc. and writing them down. We worked through the whys and our reasons for choosing what we wanted in our lives. This seminar was more than just a typical goal-setting course. It required you to look inside yourself, face your fears, find deeply personal reasons to motivate you to reach for your desires. I realized how important it was to sincerely consider the why behind each of my goals. I was so inspired and motivated throughout the course exercises that I dedicated over 3 months to complete the progam. This was a profound turning point in my life. In the end, I developed a 100-page book that listed my goals, my reasons, and my progress steps toward fulfillment. And now 3 years later, amazingly, but not surprisingly, I am well on my way to attaining those dreams that I set for myself. Although there are other great courses out there, I shamelessly recommend this one to everyone who will listen. It is listed in Chapter 7 of this book.

The point of this story is of course the power of setting intentions and defining your inner motivations to accomplish them. I also discovered that writing your goals down, especially in your own handwriting, sets your intentions more powerfully than you can imagine. Being completely honest with yourself about what you truly want for your life and why you want it is key. You do not have to conform with other people's desires, goals, and beliefs. You are an individual with your own talents and perspectives on life. You are here for a purpose, so identify that purpose (or purposes, you can have more than one) and step into it!

Have The Confidence To Ask For More

You are worthy, you are valuable, and you deserve the best life has to offer. However, oftentimes you must have the courage to ask for it. Be it a raise, a promotion, more freedom, or that special project at work. Or more assistance and respect at home. If you are not sure of the right words, talk it though with someone you trust or find a template online that you can modify to fit your circumstances. I would also like to interject a term here -- inspired action. It refers to stepping out and doing or saying something because you feel an urge, inclination, or desire to do it. We have intuitive guidance that is always leading us in the right direction on our path. When you listen to that inner voice and follow through on its guidance, you will attract the opportunities, the income, and the respect that you deserve.

Take care of your body.

Or do you not know that your body is
the temple of the Holy Spirit
who is in you, whom you have from God,
and you are not your own?

--1 Corinthians 6:19, NKJV

We interact with this world and with others through our bodies. Treating your body with respect and care includes eating healthy foods, drinking plenty of water, getting adequate sleep, exercising, and seeking preventive medical care. Stimulating your mind and senses with activity can improve brain health and mental clarity.

Specifically, the importance of sleep cannot be overemphasized. So many of us do not get the appropriate amount of sleep each night. We find many excuses not to go to bed too early ("I need to work on this just a little longer" or "I can't go to sleep until this task is completed.") or, due to inner chaos, we have trouble falling asleep or staying asleep. Sometimes health issues create disruptive sleep patterns. We all know proper rest is essential for good mental and physical health, mood, and maintaining high energy levels throughout the day. If your sleep habits are not consistent or mental stress and overactive thoughts are keeping you awake, obtain medical advice. Do your best to go to bed at the same time each night and wake up at the same time every morning. Ensure that you are sleeping the correct number of hours for your body to feel refreshed and to maximize the benefits. Train your body and mind to develop proper sleep habits and you will be amazed at how much better you <u>feel</u> and how troublesome aspects of your life become clearer and more easily managed with a fresh outlook each day.

Make Time For Prayer and Meditation

In our technology-driven society, there is a lot that clamors for our attention. We often get sucked into social media, mainstream TV media, video games, and the like. It is not wrong; however, we need to recognize that our minds can be overwhelmed with voices, data, and experiences outside of ourselves that divert us from our true priorities. Sometimes silence is the best answer.

Meditation is a personal devotion or mental exercise that deepens self-awareness and minimizes reactions to negative thoughts. The word "meditation" derives from the Latin word "meditari" and means to reflect, think, and contemplate. The practice of meditating can quiet the mind and silence thought, allowing inner self introspection. Prayer, on the other hand, is communication with a higher power. It is different from meditation as it is not passive reflection; it is a direct petition to God. These definitions are provided to clarify the two internal practices that can help us transcend our chaotic environment. Carving out time each day, even just for 15 minutes, for meditation and prayer can transform your life. It is extremely helpful to learn how to dial down the energy of the mind.

I was raised in a religious family and prayer was part of our daily routine. Due to my beliefs, I was comfortable making requests and expressing my thankfulness to God. Until I began to study meditation, I did not realize the differences and the need for both. Meditation takes practice, but when you can employ it successfully even for a few minutes, it is life changing. Quieting the mind and turning off thought opens the door to mental clarity and improving intuition. I cannot begin to express all of the improvements I have noticed in my attitude, my mood, my faith, and the serendipitous experiences that have entered my life.

There are many wonderful, validated courses online and in-person that teach meditation principles. I have included some in Chapter 7 to get you started. Remember, anything worth doing takes practice. Consistency is key. And you do not have to be perfect (and you won't be) to witness the transformation that meditation and prayer bring into your life. Try it. You will become a believer too.

When Something Makes You Feel Happy, Do It As Often As Possible

When you are able give attention and energy toward those things that you find pleasurable, that calm you, that bring joy into your day, it reinforces the idea that you are consciously choosing to be happy. When a thought or an action brings a smile to your face, linger on it, take an extra moment to relish it and appreciate it. It is said that it takes 21 days to form a habit, which means your mind needs consistent repetitive thoughts and actions that "program" it. Give it positive reinforcement. In a matter of a few weeks, your feelings about yourself and your life will change. Create your "happy habit".

Once you begin prioritizing self-love and reaching for your inner happiness, <u>life around you</u> will begin to change for the better also. Ideas and opportunities will flow, and you will notice them because of your increased self-awareness. People and situations will look different because your perspective has changed. As the inner work progresses, taking stock and consciously making changes to your daily family and work routines will be a natural next step. The next chapter provides tried and tested ideas for just that…

Chapter 3 Organizing Your Life

"Being organized isn't about getting rid of everything you own
or trying to become a different person:
it's about living the way you want to live, but better."
—Andrew Mellen

As a working mother, it can feel like you are being pulled in many directions all at the same time. You would love to make more time to enjoy yourself with your family, and at the same time you do not want to lose focus on your career, and those clothes need washing, and dinner needs to be cooked, and an extended family member just requested a ride to the doctor's office. Managing all that life throws your way daily can be overwhelming!

Even though you are in a constant state of motion, it can also feel like you are not able to get everything done. New responsibilities and tasks continue to pop up from every angle. Shifting priorities and emotional demands, at home and at work, pull at you from all sides. It can become frustrating and exhausting.

We often view those that seem to "have it all" as superhuman. A thriving marriage, a lucrative career, well-adjusted children. How do they do it?? Successfully mastering the art and science of balance and productivity is possible. Remember, everyone has the same hours in a day. There is no such thing as a one-size-fits-all perfect solution to create a balanced and productive life. It's personal, and each person has different needs and priorities. However, there are resources and short-cuts that can help.

The Key Is Organization!

Choosing where you spend your time directly impacts the sense of balance in your life. Time management begins and ends with organization. <u>Making the time to properly organize your life can be game-changing</u>. And "making the time" is a critical phrase in this statement. If you find yourself running around in circles, jumping from task to task, and without enough time to complete any of them, then take a hard look at your priorities and time management. Lack of organization leaves you unfocused and easily distracted or trying to multi-task many duties at once. And you end up anxious, frazzled, and easily triggered. When you are organized, you have a routine, you are aware of upcoming responsibilities and events, and true priorities will automatically start rising to the top. You will feel more in control, successful, and productive. Your family will notice and will be influenced by your new-found sense of balance and control.

It is important to do first things first – and this includes organizing your life. Booking an appointment with yourself, setting aside the time (and honoring it!), to do the work of consciously reviewing who, what, where, when, and how you spend your time is eye-opening! From there, you can identify the priorities, the time-wasters, and determine an organizational strategy that works for you. Some ideas to consider when you begin this work:

1. Choose to Act <u>Intentionally</u>

Keeping the bigger picture in mind is important. And it helps to establish the structure of priorities. Understanding the "why" behind your decisions and actions is critical to ensure that they are aligned with you, and your family's, long-term goals. Why am I doing this right now? Is it necessary in this moment, or should it be addressed later? How important is it? We often get swept up into action without a thought as to its true importance in the bigger picture. We spend a lot of time on things that do not have a positive ROI – return on investment, time investment in this case. When you can strategically identify necessary action items versus time wasters in relation to your short and long-range goals and desired outcomes, you become more purposeful and intentional in all of your actions.

2. Consciously Set Your Priorities

Building on the intentional action concept, prioritizing tasks and responsibilities is the next step of organized and balanced living. When creating a to-do list, for example, setting the highest priorities in order of importance and the associated time commitments for each can help you focus on one task at a time until each is completed. And you are less likely to get side-tracked because you have consciously identified the importance of the task at hand.

To keep the big picture in mind, ask yourself an important question: "If I can only complete one thing today, what would it be?" The answer becomes the top of your priority list. And then ask that same question again: "If I could only complete 2 things today, what would the second one be?" Continue the process until you have each item on your list in order based on importance and time. If a task is left uncompleted at the end of the day, in most cases, it can be prioritized into the next day. No worries!

If an obligation arises that is not on your prioritized list, unless it is an emergency, you can make a note of it and return to it at an appropriate designated time. In this way, you are more likely to stay on task and not be distracted to venture off into actions that have a lower ROI in the present moment.

3. The Family Calendar

Keeping track of events, appointments, responsibilities, and commitments, and communicating them, is much easier on a centralized family calendar. It can be an electronic calendar, a wall calendar, or a desk calendar – any type will work as long as it is accessible to everyone and is kept up to date. Highlighting priority items on the calendar will draw your eye to them on first glance and thus reinforce the importance of these events or obligations. This one idea can minimize stress, misunderstandings, and forgotten obligations. A family calendar is a must.

4. De-Clutter Your Home

This is an item that may surprise you at first, however, when you consider its implications, it can have a huge impact on being organized and productive. Clutter and physical disorganization in a home space can create stress and wasted time. Think about "Where did I put my car keys?" and the impact a cluttered space versus an organized space could have on finding those car keys. If your home needs re-organized, start small. One room at a time. Consider donating your old books and the kids' toys that they have outgrown to a local shelter or daycare facility. Begin practicing the art of giving away one item every day or every week to declutter your home and workspace. Even a weekend de-clutter project such as cleaning out the garage (with everyone contributing to the goal) can set a standard of tidiness and productivity for the family. It is amazing how good it makes you feel when even a small project is completed!

5. *Ask For Help*

So many of us have the mindset that we need to do most things on our own. We have trained ourselves to be independent. "It's just easier if I do it" or we automatically launch into taking care of a need without considering that someone else could do it or assist us. Asking for help can be difficult and uncomfortable for many of us. It is important to understand that it is okay to ask for help from those who can give it and who can support us. Recognize that sharing responsibilities creates a healthy balance. It does not have to be all on your shoulders. And sharing duties also benefits others. They become more involved, have an opportunity to learn new skills, and feel the reward of contributing to the family. So, take your sister up on her offer to babysit one night. Ask your kids to help with the dishes or the laundry. Talk to your spouse about hiring a housekeeper or a yard maintenance company to tackle those tasks more efficiently. It should not surprise you at how much more productive you can become when you stop trying to do everything by yourself!

My home is my sanctuary. And I love, and must have, a meticulously clean home space. It's just my thing and makes me feel good. I also travel quite often in my career. I was finding that keeping the house dusted and mopped was a challenge for me. The smaller chores, washing dishes, doing laundry, making up beds, minimizing clutter, I could complete fairly easily. It was the house cleaning part that I often didn't have time to undertake. And, plus, certain chores I really disliked – scrubbing bathtubs and toilets and mopping floors – yuk. When these chores were not getting done regularly, it would cause me anxiety and stress. I finally decided that I needed a housekeeper to come twice per month to do the heavy lifting. I reached out, interviewed, and assessed the ROI of incurring the expense versus the time and stress it would save me, and it was a win-win. It was the right decision for me and, to this day, the toilets and the floors I leave to someone else to take care of.

6. Balance Organization and Flexibility

This may sound counter-intuitive, but you should not be so organized that you become inflexible. You should always create a little room in your life for the unexpected. Most working mothers who seem like they have it all together and are super organized share this little secret. Not everything can be controlled. Allowing new things to enter your experience keeps life interesting anyway! You identify, prioritize, and focus on the events and duties that you are aware of, and you accept that there will be those things that will surprise you. And when they do, then you then have a choice to make. Is it of enough priority to address it now? And sometimes it is. Other times, it is a task or commitment that is more beneficial to be delayed. Staying flexible and being able to shift priorities occasionally is key to your productivity and to your sanity.

Improving your organizational skills will aid you in making more progress, with less stress, in your daily responsibilities and with that never-ending to-do list. Productivity begins with identifying the needs, setting the priorities, and establishing a plan and timeline for each. And then, of course, consistently working that plan through successful completion. You are not required to change everything all at once to see tangible results. As you make changes to your lifestyle, your thoughts, and daily actions incrementally, you can build upon each success. Begin with just one of these ideas today and your life, and your family's life, will begin to change for the better.

Chapter 4 Productivity Tips & Tricks

> *"Perfection is not attainable,*
> *but if we chase perfection*
> *we can catch excellence."*
>
> --Vince Lombardi

Your mindset is one-half the battle and organization is the other half. As we discussed in the last chapter, being organized and deliberate is the platform on which productivity is based. Thoughtless constant action to make things happen and get things done is not necessarily productive. Once you have become better organized, the following tips and ideas will enhance success and ultimate balance across your home and work lives.

Start The Day Right

As a busy mother and professional, it can be a herculean task to find time for yourself. Chances are that even when you do manage to find a few minutes to yourself, you may begin feeling guilty because you know that responsibilities and duties remain undone. Start your day right by practicing self-care, with no guilt. As we have already discussed, if you are emotionally or physically exhausted, you cannot take care of others or complete those important items on your to-do list. It bears repeating -- you have to choose yourself as a priority also.

One option: Begin your day by waking early, 15-30 minutes before the rest of the family rises, to guarantee some time to yourself. Contemplating the upcoming day and consciously placing it in perspective can have valuable benefits. You can use these early minutes of the day to do the following:

- Watch the sun rise
- Read a chapter of your book while sipping a cup of coffee
- Write in your journal
- Meditate or pray
- Exercise

Even just 15 minutes of solitude and quiet can start your day off on the right note and set you on the path of productivity and balance. Remember, YOU set the tone and attitude for your day.

Write It Down

It seems obvious, but keeping a written list works wonders for identifying priorities and focusing attention. But some do not take the time to do it. Why? There are many ways to document your tasks and projects – electronically in Microsoft Outlook for example, in a journal, a written to-do list, or on the family calendar that we spoke of in the last chapter. Find a simple solution that works best for you. Prepare your list for the next day the evening before. Review it again in the morning as a reminder and to set the intentions for the day.

It may be helpful to limit the daily to-do list to a manageable 3-5 items per day, taking into consideration your work hours, your home hours, and the types of obligations themselves. Share the list with your family to ensure everyone is reminded of the day's duties and events and their timing.

Balance Difficult Tasks With Easier Ones

To maximize productivity, set the order of the various tasks that should be completed today. Often, it works to your mental benefit to approach the easier and less time-consuming tasks first. This way there are some immediate successes which will drive your motivation to continue through your list. Clearly identify the hardest and most time-consuming tasks and ensure that appropriate amounts of time are set aside for them during the day. Balance the easy with the hard, the fun and comfortable with the unpleasant. Take turns – do an easier task, then tackle a harder task. This may not always be the best approach depending on the to-do list items or how the day actually unfolds, but it is worth considering.

"Multi-tasking", or performing several tasks at the same time, is technically not valid according to scientific brain research. However, allowing technology to help you do multiple tasks simultaneously is valid. For example, as the clothes are washing in the washing machine, you can make a grocery store run or help the kids with their homework. With the current state of programmable technology, you can set scheduled reminders, turn the oven on and off, and unlock your house or car doors. Use this technology to your advantage to maximize your time and simplify your tasks where you can.

Learn To Say No

The Balancing Act of A Busy Mom

A friend of mine called one morning and invited my husband and I to a dinner party that same night. She "threw it together" on short notice since her and her husband found themselves with a free evening. My husband and I had had a particularly difficult week and were hoping for a quiet evening at home with the kids. However, I felt a little guilty because we hadn't gotten together with our friends in quite a while, so I convinced my husband to go. We had to secure a last-minute babysitter and pick up an hors d'oeuvre to bring with us. So, by the time we entered the party, we felt frazzled and tired, but we pasted smiles on our faces anyway. It was a delightful atmosphere, but we did not fully enjoy it because our hearts were not truly in it. We counted the minutes until we could excuse ourselves to come home. As I thought about it later, I wished we had not gone.

We all have similar stories like this. We have had difficulty at times saying no to last-minute requests or to those that deliberately cornered us to ask for help. We ended up with obligations that we did not expect (and didn't have time for) or at events where we did not really want to be. And then what happens? We do not give our best, we don't always fulfill the promises that we made, and we feel resentful. This is not healthy, and it does not serve anyone! You <u>can</u> say no, respectfully and directly, without sounding harsh or selfish. It is critical that we all learn to do so. You cannot be everything to everybody and you cannot be everywhere at any given time.

"I am not able to work that into my schedule today."

"I am not feeling up to it tonight. Let's plan to do that at another time."

"I am busy this afternoon. I cannot take care of that for you today."

Sometimes it is best to say no. And we do not have to apologize for it. I realized I should have said no to my friend's party, not only for my friends' sake (we were not in the right frame of mind to enjoy it with her), for my poor husband's sake, and for my own.

Recognize Interdependence

Why do we, as women in particular, often feel we have to do everything ourselves? Maybe we give people the impression that we *want* to do everything and *can* do anything, so they let us do it. Independence is a valued quality, but too much of a good thing can have the opposite effect. Others become trained that you will always take care of things and then they may choose not to step up or try to do things for themselves. This can become detrimental when it comes to our kids. Children need to learn independence, but how can they when a parent takes care of everything for them?!

Let's try <u>interdependence</u>. Allow others to contribute. Teach children the skills they will need as they grow up. Request help and support from your spouse or partner. Tap into other people's strengths and expertise. "Well, they will not do it like I do it." So what? As long as the outcome is acceptable, does it matter the path?

I believe there is a trait that many of us have that interferes with interdependence: the need for control. If we are honest with ourselves, we know this to be true. This deep-rooted need often drives perfectionism. We feel we are the only ones that can do a certain task and do it "right" – according to our standards. We subconsciously pressure ourselves and bear many more responsibilities than we need to under the guise of martyrdom. This belief is unfair (and also quite pretentious) to others and to ourselves. Most duties and projects can succeed just as well in others' hands as our own. We must find the courage to release control and allow interdependence.

Unplug From Social Media

Social media is an amazing tool to stay in touch with friends and stay up to date on those people, places, and things that interest you. And, of course, your cellphone is a must-have these days. It is technology, like we discussed earlier, so it can be used for task management, reminders, and checking email while riding the train to the office, for example. Used wisely, it can increase productivity. However, as we all know, it can also be a timewaster and create procrastination. It can be a huge distraction when you are trying to stay focused on a project. Honestly evaluate the amount of time you spend on the phone and how you are using it. Checking email or posting to twitter or snapchat? Is it really productive time? Advice: Schedule time to put it down.

Research has shown a dramatic decline in closeness, communication, and intimacy when the phone is in your hand while you are talking to and interacting with those around you. Even if you are not using it! Others may feel less acknowledged and that your electronic connection is more important than they are in that moment. And sometimes they are right, aren't they? This is an area that I actually got called out on. And it really brought to my attention how I was not in the moment when I really needed to be. It was after work hours and I was waiting for an important work email to arrive that I felt I needed to address immediately. I was sitting with my son on our patio swing and he was telling me about his day. I was listening, but I was also looking at my phone every few minutes to make sure I hadn't missed any incomings. This went on for several minutes until, exasperated, he placed his hands on either side of my face and, looking me straight in the eye, said "Mommy, I'm right here. Are you listening?" He was seven years old at the time. Needless to say, it was another lightbulb moment that hit me hard. I decided to spend those precious present moments engaging with my son. The work email would just have to wait.

It was a lesson in BEING PRESENT. Whatever you are doing, be present in the moment for it. Your phone and social media can absolutely aid you, but they can also distract you. It is amazing how productive you can be when you remain focused and uninterrupted on the task, the conversation, and the work at hand.

Exercise For At least 20 Minutes Each Day

This may seem an odd addition to a chapter on productivity but let me persuade you that it belongs here. As we all know, there are numerous benefits of consistent exercise. Stress reduction, energy boosts, and better health have direct impacts on mood, mental clarity, and pursuing your goals in life.

My co-workers often chuckle at me when they find me walking the hallway or the stairs at work. When I have something on my mind that I need to think through, I will get up out of my chair and go for a walk. Moving my body, even for a few minutes, clears my mind and helps me to think. And I always feel better, more uplifted, after I have taken the time to do it. So, making time in your day to walk, take the stairs, play tennis, yoga, dance, whatever raises your heart rate, is an effort toward self-care and a step toward inner happiness. Science has shown exercise reduces stress response in the body and improves mental clarity. It increases your energy level so you will have the stamina and strength to finish what you start. Just do it!

Face the Hard Things

There will always be experiences, issues, and tasks that we do not want to address or make a decision about. We often refuse to look at the hard stuff or place it on a back burner. And most of the time those things do not get better with age. Face it, do it, finish it. Cultivate an attitude of courage and resilience by choosing to "bite the bullet" and address the hardest, thankless responsibilities and problems as soon as you can. It takes guts, focus, and perseverance to pick them up, work through them, and resolve them. You have what it takes. Tackle an outstanding task or issue every day for the next week and take stock of how you feel when you do!

Reward Yourself For Task Completion

The idea here is to celebrate the wins, even the small ones. With every task you complete, reward yourself. Maybe that means you put your feet up for 15 minutes, have a cup of tea, color with your children, have that ice cream treat, or make plans for that date night. Simple "pats on the back" acknowledge your successes and motivate you to strike the balance between getting things done and resetting your energy. Try this: Separate your tasks into 30-minute work bursts balanced with 10-minute breaks. Set a timer. Stay focused for 30 minutes and then allow the breaks in between to be used for moments of fun and upliftment. This helps create the habit of balance. Also, do your best to experience as much joy as possible when performing your tasks and that alone will make you feel much happier, more productive and accomplished at the end of the day.

Say No to Guilt

Guilt is one of the easiest traps to fall into, and it is one of the most demoralizing feelings we can have. It is so easy to feel like we do not do enough for our kids, our spouse or partner, and our extended families when we are balancing the requirements of a career with our family obligations. Be kind to yourself. Being hard on yourself, or allowing others to plant the seeds of guilt, may force us to change our priorities, but not always for the right reasons. Be aware of those tender areas in your life that seem to create guilt within you. Ask yourself why. What is the trigger? What types of situations make me feel this way? If you need to, talk to someone, a counselor for example, that can help you view those situations in a more positive manner. If someone in your life is trying to guilt-trip you into making certain decisions, recognize it for what it is and choose not to internalize it. Those lovely people are coming to you from a place of selfishness – they want you to agree with them or do something that will meet <u>their</u> need. You can respectfully say no and choose not to give in to the guilt.

Remember, maintain perspective. Maybe the trash is not always taken out on time. Maybe the laundry is left unfolded for a day or two. Maybe the dishes are not always washed and put away. It does not have to be perfect to be effective.

That goes for most things in life. No one can be, do, and have everything at all times. Manage your expectations. You <u>are</u> doing many things right.

Network With Positive Working Mothers

Surround yourself with other working mothers where you all can share and support each other. Creating connections with neighborhood families, co-workers at the workplace, parents at daycare, school, or church groups can provide mental and emotional support when needed. You can learn from each other. Online resources across many platforms, such as parenting seminars, podcasts, and community groups, are also available. Be sure that the people you choose to interact with have positive attitudes and manage their lives with grace and accountability, like you are trying to do.

Chase Perfection; Catch Excellence

Revisiting one of my favorite quotes from the beginning of this chapter, Vince Lombardi was wise, and he was right. Perfection is not humanly possible, however if we set our standards high and consistently strive towards them, we can build lives of excellence. Recognizing that you cannot control every aspect of life that surrounds you, but you can choose how you react to it is an eye-opening realization. Ultimately, our outer worlds are a reflection of our inner worlds. If our minds and hearts are full of chaos, fear, and guilt, then our daily lives will be filled with stress, conflict, and unnecessary drama. If we make the choice to fill ourselves from the inside with peace, reason, and grace, then our daily lives will play out in a very different manner reflecting what is within. Accept that you cannot control everything and that it is okay. Set your intentions, follow through, react from a place of inner awareness, and keep the big picture in mind.

To live an intentional and productive life is a choice. While it may not be perfectly blended and balanced all of the time, that is fine. Balance feeds productivity. The moment you harness the power of balance, you begin to focus on creating productivity in your life.

Happiness, balance, and productivity go hand in hand. It takes focus and effort to identify, prioritize, and organize. It is also just as important to take care of yourself, so that you have the health, the energy, and the clarity of thought to set the tone of your own home and workplace. The more intentional you become, the more balanced you become and thus, the more productive you become. Finding and nurturing your happiness is the ultimate success.

Chapter 5 The Benefits of Balance

"No person, no place, and no thing has any power over us,
for 'we' are the only thinkers in our mind.
When we create peace and harmony and balance in our minds,
we will find it in our lives.
--Louise L. Hay

The balancing act of a career mom is a continuous cycle of doing, reflecting, re-prioritizing, and refining. It is not a one and done achievement – once you've figured it out, you have it made– because life is always in a state of change and evolution. As we discussed earlier, flexibility and adaptation are traits to embrace because you will always need them.

There will be times, and plenty of them, when you will need to take a step back and reassess your activities, your

The Benefits of Balance

thoughts, your health and wellbeing. What is currently causing me stress, imbalance, or feelings of dissatisfaction? How is this situation affecting my home life and/or my job performance? What are my priorities in this moment? Am I compromising? When you can acknowledge the answers to these questions then you can begin to address them.

There is a beautiful and simple resource called the Life Balance Wheel or The Wheel of Life that provides insight into the areas of your life that are flourishing and those that may be struggling. It helps to guide you toward breaking down barriers and identifying the changes that may be needed to improve balance and fulfillment. The Life Balance Wheel is a practical tool that anyone can use to assess life satisfaction and set goals that are aligned with deeply held core values. A link is included in the last chapter of this book.

Interestingly, once you begin to become more self-aware and know what balance feels like, when you start to wander off balance or become less productive, you will notice it. Pay attention to how you feel and the emotions that bubble to the surface. If you perform frequent emotional self-assessments, you can catch when things begin to shift toward unbalance. And you can be more proactive in addressing it.

Having this awareness can help you to feel less stressed overall. Stressors at home and at work can accumulate over time and trigger burnout. Striving for balance has direct positive effects on mental health. The risk of health conditions needing medical intervention are also reduced when those stresses are minimized and managed appropriately.

Additionally, when we have a more balanced family and work life it becomes easier to manage our time. Everyone has 24 hours in a day, but how they choose to spend it differs enormously! Allocating time more effectively we can "make" the time we need to handle both personal and work matters without sacrifice.

The Fear of Missing Out (FOMO) has been documented as a real mental disorder. It stems from anxiety at the thought of being excluded from an event or experience or not being "in the know" about someone or something. When life is balanced, there is time to have a life within the home, at the workplace, and as part of outside social groups, so you are less likely to feel FOMO.

Mindfulness is an important component of life balance creation. As we move through life intentionally, we often naturally develop a greater control over our <u>focus</u>. This has a huge impact on our concentration and the ability to minimize reactions to distractions that can take us off course. Being more present in the moment and the ability to identify those people, things, and experiences that are truly meaningful to your life has its own rewards.

An obvious, but sometimes overlooked, outcome is the pleasure of improved relationships. When we run ourselves ragged every day, we often do not have nurturing family time or personal time with our spouses or partners. We can be physically together but so often our minds are still "out there" ruminating on other issues. Remember the story about my son and I in Chapter 4. A balanced lifestyle accommodates <u>quality</u> time with family and friends.

As we have been discussing happiness, organization, and productivity throughout this book, it should be no secret by now that balanced individuals are more motivated and productive. So many times we think, erroneously, that taking action, doing more, working around the clock means being more productive. It has been proven scientifically that it is the other way around! Balancing working and downtime, completing tasks and then enjoying the rewards of those successes, and allowing for flexible time management at home and at work all contribute to deep inner motivation and fulfillment, which in turn creates higher levels of productivity.

There is no one-size-fits-all perfect formula to create balance and productivity as a working mother in this day and age. However, by contemplating, internalizing, and applying simple yet proven ideas that ring true for you, improvements can begin today. The benefits are real, valuable, and will continue to grow as you repeat and refine those practices that work best for you.

Chapter 6 Conclusions and Insights

"The purpose of our life is to be happy."

—Dalai Lama

Little did I know how these principles would change my life. As a single mother of two young boys with a thriving career, my divided focus often made me feel overwhelmed and exhausted, like I was not doing enough and doing too much at the same time. I felt I had little control over my time. And doing things for myself? Well, that was completely out of the question!

But I was open. I knew things needed to change. I was unhappy, and that HAD to change. In desperation, and through much prayer, I believe these concepts and ideas, taken from many sources, were some of the answers that I needed. It took me a few years, but I have applied every single one of them and I can tell you that my life has become

Conclusions & Insights

more stable, balanced and productive. And most importantly of all, happy! I vowed to help other women like me by sharing concepts like self-love, meditation, intentional prioritization, and tips for personal productivity that they could incorporate into their busy lives to radically change their work-life balance for the better and create lasting fulfillment and happiness for themselves and their families.

In summary,

» Your personal happiness is valuable and necessary. It is the key and the first step to finding your inner balance which will begin to create the outer balance in your life experience.

» When you understand what self-love actually is, what it isn't, and how to apply it to yourself, the changes to your thinking and your beliefs can be transformative.

» Time management begins and ends with organization. Applying simple, proven approaches will assist you in prioritizing your tasks and organizing your days and that will change your life.

- » The highlighted actionable productivity principles dovetail into and extend the reach of your organizational techniques. They can positively affect your mindset so every day becomes more and more productive.

- » The benefits of happiness and balance are obvious: less stress, more quality time, improved relationships, and increased productivity. Conscious self-awareness is the key to maintaining balance – when you recognize immediately that you are out of balance you can then take steps to correct it.

Many of the concepts presented here may be new to you, as they were for me at one time. They may seem strange or counter-intuitive. I thought so too. And you may not believe that they can actually make that much of a difference. Ditto again. Or maybe you have heard of some of them but didn't really know what they meant or had little motivation to find out. If you are at a place in your life right now where the rat race is too much, you are wearing yourself out trying to juggle everything on your plate from day to day, and your happiness

Conclusions & Insights

with it all is fleeting, I urge you take the ideas presented here seriously and test them out for yourself.

<u>Where</u> do you start improving your life? At the beginning – with your own happiness. Which ideas and concepts of this book inspired you the most? Begin incorporating those ideas into your routine. <u>When</u> do you start improving your life? Right now. In this moment. Act on one idea from this book that resonated with you, and consciously dedicate yourself to it, and then examine the results. All you need is one inspired action, even seemingly small, and it can grow to change your life. As you have seen, the concepts build on each other, so the flow from one inspired idea to the next will be natural. Happiness feeds balance which feeds productivity.

Once you begin to understand and allow yourself to internalize these principles, more ideas and desire to continue this journey will unfold. When you experience the positive outcomes from applying these principles, then you will know that there is no going back to the way things once were. And you wouldn't want to anyway!

Always remember, YOU have the power to create your own happiness, improve your work-life balance, and have the daily productivity you desire. It is possible. And you were meant to have it.

Chapter 7 Continue Your Progress

"Change is inevitable.
Growth is optional."
--John Maxwell

The age of technology is a wonderful thing! There are many courses, websites, blogs, and videos that provide outstanding and inspiring content that can aid you in your journey. Additional resources can empower you in continuing your growth toward lasting happiness, balance, and productivity. It is a lifelong journey. One with twists and turns, highs and lows, but worth it all the same.

The first few resources listed are those that were specifically identified throughout this book. Additional support for the content contained in this book is listed under References.

Mindvalley Lifebook Course:

https://www.mindvalley.com/lifebook/online

Meditation Practitioners and Courses:

- Basics of Meditation: Mindful Meditation with Deepak Chopra (The Chopra Foundation) https://chopra.com/online-courses/meditation-foundations
- The M Word by Emily Fletcher (Mindvalley) https://www.mindvalley.com/mword/masterclass
- 30-Day Mindfulness Course (School of Positive Transformation) https://schoolofpositivetransformation.com/positive-mindfulness-program/

The Wheel of Life Tool:

https://www.mindtools.com/ak6jd6w/the-wheel-of-life

References by Chapter:

Chapter 1

1. Definitions of happiness:

    https://www.dictionary.com/browse/happiness;

    https://www.merriam-webster.com/dictionary/happiness

2. Abundance mentality:

https://www.happiness.com/magazine/science-psychology/abundance-mindset/;

https://www.verywellmind.com/how-to-shift-from-a-scarcity-mindset-to-an-abundance-mindset-5220862

3. Positive thinking and affirmations:

   https://www.mayoclinic.org/healthy-lifestyle/stress-management/in-depth/positive-thinking/art-20043950;

   https://theblissfulmind.com/positive-affirmations-list/

4. The laws of frequency and attraction:

   https://www.youtube.com/watch?v=XEX2-m8EabU

   https://www.mindbodygreen.com/articles/law-of-vibration

Chapter 2

5. Definitions of self-love:

   https://www.merriam-webster.com/dictionary/self-love;

   https://psychcentral.com/blog/imperfect/2019/05/what-is-self-love-and-why-is-it-so-important

6. Multi-tasking:

   https://health.clevelandclinic.org/science-clear-multitasking-doesnt-work/;

   https://www.science.org/content/article/multitasking-splits-brain

7. Martyr syndrome:

    https://www.healthline.com/health/martyr-complex#martyr-vs-victim

    https://www.youtube.com/watch?v=sxNzA84daLc

8. Inspired Action:

    https://exploringyourmind.com/inspired-action-what-it-is-and-how-to-implement-it/

9. Meditation:

    https://www.psychologytoday.com/us/basics/meditation;

    https://www.youtube.com/watch?v=hxRpvEkKzTA

10. Prayer:

    https://www.gotquestions.org/what-is-prayer.html

Chapter 3

11. The deeper work involved in time management:

    https://hbr.org/2020/01/time-management-is-about-more-than-life-hacks

12. Organized at work:

    https://asana.com/resources/get-organized

13. Organized at Home:

https://ourhappyhive.com/the-best-home-management-tips/

Chapter 4

14. Additional Productivity Tips:

    https://www.realsimple.com/work-life/life-strategies/how-to-be-productive

Chapter 5

15. Benefits of life balance:

    https://positivepsychology.com/what-is-work-life-balance/

    https://qiii.media/6-reasons-why-a-good-life-balance-is-important-for-you/

16. Fear of missing out (FOMO):

    https://www.wellandgood.com/fomo-mental-health-condition/

17. Work-life balance improves productivity:

    https://hbr.org/2022/09/the-surprising-benefits-of-work-life-support

About The Author

Melissa Harris, CRM, CIC, COSS, is a CEO-Director of a large public entity risk management organization, where she has established a culture of leading-edge innovation with uncompromising integrity, and mentored team members to greater heights in their abilities and personal fulfillment in their contributions. She has spent the last several years refining organizational leadership, developing high performing staff, and promoting exceptional customer service for clients. She is also an experienced public speaker, actor, and business entrepreneur.

Her passions include researching and writing about personal development in the areas of business, leadership, spirituality, and living your best life. She believes everyone is born with a purpose and we are called to inspire each other to embrace our gifts and share them with the world.

Follow:
www.amazon.com/author/myclearvision_mharris
www.linkedin.com/in/melissaschlattharris-1clrvsn

Other Books From This Author:

Leading With Empathy In A Remote Work World

About The Publisher

The mission of Vue Claire is to publish, market, and promote written, video and audio works that encourage personal and professional development in the areas of business, leadership, life skills, and spirituality.

More Information

If you enjoyed this work, please leave a review.
Reviews help spread the word that this content is useful
and can positively impact more lives.

Questions?

Contact the Author/Publisher: Vue.claire.llc@gmail.com

<u>Other Books From This Publisher</u>:

Anime Art Interactive Journal

Anime Art My Dreams Journal

Anime Art Anime Princesses Coloring Book

Anime Art Victorian Steampunk Anime Coloring Book Vol. 1

Anime Art Victorian Steampunk Anime Coloring Book Vol. 2

Anime Art In The City Anime Coloring Book

Anime Art Wedding Day Dreams Anime Coloring Book

Anime Art Color-Sketch-Journal Anime Activity Book

My Sarcastic Life Coloring Book

My Sarcastic Life Coloring Book

Mommy & Me Queens and Princesses Coloring Book

Dad & Me Dinosaurs and Cool Cars Coloring Book

Magical Mandalas Color By Number Coloring Book

Anime Art Warrior Men Anime & Fantasy Portraits Coloring Book

Anime Art Angelic Chibi Anime Princess Coloring Book Vol. 1

Le Mandala Noir Coloring Book

Anime Art Anime Activity Book --
Learn Japanese - Wordsearch Puzzles - Coloring Pages

Modern Art Flowing Patterns Coloring Book

www.ingramcontent.com/pod-product-compliance
Lightning Source LLC
Chambersburg PA
CBHW020654060526
44119CB00068B/2